MUSE

❖

JOSEPH FAGAN

Belfast
LAPWING

First Published by Lapwing Publications
c/o 1, Ballysillan Drive
Belfast BT14 8HQ
lapwing.poetry@ntlworld.com
http://www.lapwingpoetry.com

Copyright © Joseph Fagan 2014

All rights reserved
The author has asserted her/his right under Section 77
of the Copyright, Design and Patents Act 1988
to be identified as the author of this work.
British Library Cataloguing in Publication Data.
A catalogue record for this book is available from
the British Library.

Since before 1632
the Greig sept of the MacGregor Clan
has been printing and binding books

Lapwing Publications are printed and
hand-bound in Belfast at the Winepress.
Set in Aldine 721 BT

ISBN 978-1-909252-72-1

ACKNOWLEDGEMENTS

Acknowledgements due to the editors of following publications in which some of these poems were first printed, also many thanks to the editors and competition judges listed below:

Café Review, USA
Acorn
Skylight Poets Galway
Tandem
Incognito
Cobweb
Norwich Writers
North Words Scotland
Rainbows & Stone Anthology

Broadcast / Discussed on a Radio Eireann Arts Programme
Poetry Ireland Review edited by Maurice Harmon
Poetry Ireland Review Edited by Moya Cannon
Poetry Ireland Review Edited by Maire Mhac an tSaoi
Cuirt Journal – Editor Charlie McBride

Received 1997 Incognito Literary Award
Highly Commended by George Szirtes in 2006
Awarded category 1st Prize by George Szirtes –
Norwich Poetry 2013
Awarded 3rd Prize by Bernard O'Donoghue in
Open Competition by Tandem Poetry

CONTENTS

MUSE 1   7

Muse 1	9
Chernobyl Rose	10
Swan Song	11
A Stain on Silence	12
An Emperor called Chi	13
Corncrake	14
Little Girl Skipping	15

MUSE 2   17

Muse 2	19
As It Was In The Beginning	20
Caravaggio's The Taking of Christ	21
In His Descent...	22
Picasso's Goat	23
Our First Irises	24
In Memoriam John Reid – Aged 36	25
In Memoriam Tony Reid – aged 59	26
Survivor at Auschwitz	27
Rock Solid	28
Sun Struck	29

MUSE 3   31

Muse 3	33
Blackbird	34
A Seaside Butterfly	35
The Death of Casagemas	36
Believe Kafka	37
John Moriarty	38

The King of All the Birds	39
The Irish Mind	40
Painterly Reflections	41
The Fool's Stool	46
Goldfinch	47
The Scythe	48
Blue Blue Balloon	49
Tintinnabulation	50
Yonder	51
Arcane	51

MUSE 4   53

Muse 4	55
A la recherché du temps perdu	56
An Irish Druid asks the Trees to elect a King	57
Journey to Ithaca	58
Castaway	59
Life is a Carousel	60
Pier at Spiddal, Co. Galway	61
Rosa Lady Ardilaun	62
My Paternal Gt Grandfather Fegan's Grave Re-visited	63
The Music of Terror	64
Touchstone	65
The Sight of Death	66

To Ber,
my shadow, and our loving children -
Andrea, Barbara, Patrick, Jennifer & Veronica

JOSEPH FAGAN

MUSE 1

*M*USE

MUSE 1

My power is made perfect in weakness – 2 Cor. 12:17

Query Peace: its tenuous,
Sensuous hold on one;
Its conditional compliance:
This Micawber of movement,
This concubine of repose.

Sounds ungulate distress
The flow of calm
With visceral, untrammeled
Taunts; congeals in scary limbs
The dominance of the pack.

Immanence of fear,
Red blood of muleta,
Extemporize the fey.

*

Confront this canaille,
Leave the callejón,
Enter the arena alone.

Deny a plangent cry,
Call down from indigo sky
A steely sword.

Be El Cordobes,
El Magnifico;
Feel the blade enter,
Reducing the huge rage
To pitiable mass.

CHERNOBYL ROSE

Pink in a forest of snow,
October saw you at your best,
Fusing the long landscape with
Skies, scarlet to the rising sun.

Blooms bounce silently onto the
White breast of Mother Earth,
Tenderly, tearfully, touching her,
Radiating warmth to her inner core.

Black in a forest of snow,
Eighty-six saw you no more,
A new rose had taken your place,
Man-made of iron and ore.

Its life is measured in seconds,
It silently falls to the earth,
Dispersing death and destruction,
Destroying the womb of its birth.

SWAN SONG

There is a laundry called after you,
White Swan: somnolent white-sheets,
Cold-pure and guilt-purged, are freed
There to caress many a bare bottom.

I do not see you so intimately:
There is an otherworldliness
About you I cannot fathom;
Your universe is co-existent only.

Against the flow you glide with grace,
A Viking Long-Ship in miniature:
Recoiled prow; ochre-amber streaked;
Submerged oars; shields extended.

Uplifted, you beat the dense water
To softness with the hammering of
Angel's wings; shattering the mirror-
Image tranquility of High Heaven.

White Knight of lovers,
Sylph, svelte setter of the pose,
You deign ordinances, opacities;
Oozing primal instinct, knowledge.

Silently, with the washing of bodies,
Suborned, automaton-like,
Submerged, subsuming passion,
The Rites of Spring begin:

The Aspen shivers with delight
And sallow buds glow golden,
Cold water lilies turn their heads,
A heron's stare is frozen;

The act is done; new life begun;
Mind speaking to mind:
Informs.

A STAIN ON SILENCE
— Beckett

To hypnotize space, Mandelstam said,
To stab the sky, to reproach it because
It is empty, is to contend with the void.

I ink on rice paper an Aspen tree: a dome,
A cupola of shimmering green, coeval with
Its island base of river gravel and gunnera.

A tree, as spirit, indwelt thing, arises; not
Stone, but user of air and water; subject to
Fire; in tempest, clinging to Hades by its roots.

I sing in its branches; my voice trills as
A songbird at evening: each perfect note:
Modulated, remembered, ended.

I mar this image purposefully with carbon
Ink blobs; risking sacrilege, desecration.
My words become black holes; inverted.

AN EMPEROR CALLED CHI

To surround yourself in death with
Armies of clay-baked soldiers, and
Have all of your concubines who did
Not produce a son for you, entombed
Within your sarcophagus –
Is one thing.

But, to take to the mountain in old age;
Believe that you can make yourself
Eternal here on earth, if children, pure
Of heart, are sent forth to find for you,
The place where Heaven and Earth are
Joined together –
Is quite another thing altogether.

CORNCRAKE

The corncrake is a lonely
Bird. With his head down,
His "crake-crake" is clear
Evidence of a sad existence.

But buried in tall, primitive
Grasses, he finds a kind of happiness,
Elusive to others. Without it,
He is lost; liable to panic, to threat

Of extinction. I listen and identify
Him, here and there, in a long
Meadow. I sense, sometimes, where
He is liable to call next and exult that,

By chance or otherwise, I've got there
Before him. Both of us mythical and
Lost sources of fathomable courage.

LITTLE GIRL SKIPPING

– A Picasso Artefact

For her to seem alive
with a breadbasket torso
cardboard hair and
discarded shoes

– Not to be
a mere image/ a
montage/ a scaffolding
or an illusion –

Picasso uses a skipping
rope to hold together
a body

Suspended forever
betwixt and between
Gravity/ Art and Will.

Muse

JOSEPH FAGAN

MUSE 2

Muse

MUSE 2

Upon the Willow, in the midst thereof,
Hang up your Harp – Psalms 137-1

A broken-off twig, stuck into
wet ground by my father,
grew splendiferous.

Continuously it pours
down lamentation
to the water below.

Memento Mori it is saying;
Memento Mori to a stream
too indolent to listen.

   *

This *Salix Babylonica* baffles me.
But, a dove, nesting precariously
on a single egg, is unperturbed.

It invokes me to cast intellect aside
and to incline towards
imperfection and fear;

To expose my mind again to the
hazardous lure of unfounded
and ungrounded thoughts.

AS IT WAS IN THE BEGINNING

The well-cut stones
Proclaim new areas:
The Pines
The Paddocks
Galloping Green.

An equestrian, arboreal
Desire pervades suburban
Man, whose image of
Himself must reside
Always in fantasy.

I knew those fields
When they had real
Names that described
Them as belonging to
Real people; whose

Features were recorded
In ancient scripts
And tongues; whose
Genealogy is more
Detailed than mine.

Some night I will
Deface that gothic print:
Add Cemetery, Cul-de-Sac,
One-Way-Street, or some
Such nomenclature.

CARAVAGGIO'S THE TAKING OF CHRIST

It's not as I imagined Him:
The perfect man as half-woman,
With an effete look on His face,
And followers unable to
Cut off an ear, to save
Their lives.

My Jesus is on the Turin Cloth:
Masculine, all gravitas;
A crown of thorns
Pressed into his head;
A man who can stomach
Defeat; eyeball adversaries.

But this is the Jesus,
The One who said:
If thine enemy strike thee
Offer him
The other cheek –
Take the Man at His Word.

IN HIS DESCENT...

He remembers that day,
When his eyes first opened
To greenness, and
To those malachite hues – which remained –
Wheeled by his mother in a tub-like pram.

Unaware that a
War is on, he sees
Green-helmeted men
Soldering;
Willing to die.

He hears drones
Made by dragon flies;
Focuses on increasing circles
Caused by long-legged spiders
Moving on dappled water.

Sharp sounds inform him
Of men exorcising weeds
Off granite-edged paths –
Making shrill echoes that
Define clear boundaries.

Fishermen dragging a green boat,
With a few quick heaves,
Across a garlic-scented island,
Hold aloft, for him to count,
The day's catch.

But, the sight of his father –
Sawing savagely through fallen trees,
Pulled behind his boat and atop
Its almost submerged gunwales –
Comforts him back into sleep.

PICASSO'S GOAT

"I am created from nothing" – she says –
"Well, not nothing, but discarded things:
A palm frond is my spine, a wicker basket
my womb; I have ceramic jar udders and
metal genitalia; the rest of me is clamped
together bits of wood and scrap metal."

"I cannot see through my brilliant eyes
But I believe that you can."

"I suppose I am one of Picasso's women."

OUR FIRST IRISES

Something by Degas comes to mind:
Ruffled crepe to ravish the eye
Dancers only glimpsed.

Plant the rhizome mostly
Above ground, he'd said,
In rough, scratchy soil.

But their insolence
In showing their faces
Two summers later – surprised.

*

After many episodes
Of self-mutilation,
In the neglected gardens of the Asylum
In Saint-Rémy-de-Provence,

Van Gogh sits at an easel to depict a
Clump of Irises:

I experience moments of frightening intensity
When nature is so beautiful –
I am no longer sure of myself.

His last words – This sadness will last forever.

IN MEMORIAM JOHN REID – AGED 36

Walk slowly man, amidst the confusion of the day

I am a tiny light that shines:
See where I am – in your eye,
In your mind; in the broad sea

Or sky, in the blackness of night,
I wander & wink and never grow
Bright. Yet there I am in a sunflower

So big, lifting it's lanky head, opening
A lid. I colour the crows so black on
The corn; for this I live now; for this
I was born.

IN MEMORIAM TONY REID – AGED 59

Death has not required us to keep a day free – Beckett

… only to do the same old things, like
wrap your trumpet in a towel and
on yer bike, Tony.

You were the only person I knew
Who loved Sunday.

And so to Dun Laoghaire to play
The well-rehearsed tunes –
>   Memories of Dvorak
>   Festival of Bagdad
>   Hungarian March
>   Andante from Egyptian Ballet
>   Cead Mile Failte
>   Bolero
>   Begin the Beguine
>   Into the Storm
>   My Heart will Go On
>   Finale Resurgum

Then, the deathless sea for a swim
>   At The Forty Foot
>   On the journey home.

On the pier – late as usual –
You stopped to talk to a Coastguard.
Your bike fell from you
And down you went.

And the music had begun without you.

SURVIVOR AT AUSCHWITZ
– inter-alia – talks about visiting *phoney* Nazis.

It is not in their nature to listen, she said;
In this they resemble those whom they
Imitate. Real Nazis never came there.
For her it was a coming home.

The hut she was interned in, no longer
Stood; only its foundations was visible.
And, in the distance, the forest. Her voice
Belied the normal landscape portrayed.

On any one day, thousands, just off the
Trains, filled the forest – children and
Those unfit for labour. The children
Frolicked around the trees.

It looked like a holiday camp or picnic
Scene. But then they were all moved
Through a gate to the right, into a dark
Building with no windows. Some of the

Children continued picking flowers, and
Were plucked by guards who smashed
Their heads against concrete walls. One
Guard climbed onto the roof and threw

A canister of gas in through a small hole.
A faint wail could be heard; afterwards
The vile stench of human flesh burning,
Assaulted one's nostrils.

I thought of lines written by Yeats when
Composing Under Ben Bulben:
What matter though the skies drop
Fire – Children take hands & dance;
Death is a brief parting
And brief sickness.

ROCK SOLID

It fits snugly into the palm
Of my hand. It is no ordinary
Fossil, stuck forever into a slab
Or a piece of polished stone,

It is as perfectly shaped and
Absolute as a cut-off segment of
Eel on a marbled slab in a shop
Window, but flat-based below.

This base is serrated like the
Teeth of a Viking comb and, between
Some of the gaps one can insert
A piece of paper to its very core.

Some patronymic words in Latin,
May define its place in the scheme
Of things, e.g. *could slide over rock*;
Definitive like *Homo Sapiens*.

Et in saecula, saeculorum: the muse of
Faith against this object: place them,
Solomon, on the scales and try to
Gauge the measure of equilibrium.

SUN STRUCK

The day the sunflower exploded,
Everyone was caught by surprise.
It had seemed so contented
On its long stem, glowing brilliantly
Up into the clear heavens; each
Petal altering the sun's vermillion
To its own special mellow-yellow.

Then, without any sign or warning,
It burst asunder all over the place.
In a matter of hours, all that
Remained had become black and soggy;
Hanging down like a blight-struck
Potato stalk or a crazed famine victim –
Out of place in this world.

Muse

JOSEPH FAGAN

MUSE 3

Muse

MUSE 3

God, our Master, brings forth our intellects out of obscurity –

                                                              Seneca

Black on board: Blackboard;
Argent ideograms and white-chalked,
Mnemonic single characters:
I, Y-O-U, W-E, H-O-U-S-E, S-C-H-O-O-L

Soft, dusty fingerings spelt out;
Prismatic refractions of light:
A hieroglyphic grid drawn out of
And into existence

As a spark that runs through the
Stubble and moves a whole field
Z-I-P-P-I-N-G Z-I-G-Z-A-G-G-I-N-G
In a chain-reaction of desire.

            ★

Puer Aternus in nuce: all the time
In the world, or only a kingfisher's
Dart to reconcile the antinomies?

His world is spaced out, optimistic,
Three-dimensional, believable, in
Mr. Redmond's classroom in
Chapelizod National School.

He remembers this Free-State
Socrates peeling a daily apple
Into a single coil
Of remembered perfection.

BLACKBIRD

You sing atop my tree as if your heart is on fire.
Your food is not golden honey but earth worms.
You sing as if there is no tomorrow.
Do you not know how much my heart aches?
Someone created eternity for me. And you?
You know tomorrow only as another sunrise.

A SEASIDE BUTTERFLY

It ascended from the cover
of warm marram grass –

Two fragile, transparent wings – filigree-thin –
moving erratically above foaming crests of
incoming Atlantic rollers & held precariously
aloft by some unseen, kinematic dynamism.

I observed the impossible into oblivion.

– And oblivion is not a state like death is! –

THE DEATH OF CASAGEMAS

Nothing here is distorted.
Death is its own definition:
The self-inflicted wound,
So well-intentioned.

The vaginal flame –
Incandescent
Inextinguishable.

BELIEVE KAFKA

Bow down before enigmas/
Settle into self as into an Asylum/

Display a capacity to endure/
Be brave – if you can –/ Forget
whatever you have overcome/

Imagine freedom to be a right/
Love not a duty/

Begin each day even if it has
a meaningful golden dawning.

JOHN MORIARTY i.m. –1938-2007–

I'm on the Sky Road in Connemara with
"A Man Walking behind Cows"* to
contend with.

He confides in me that
his ploughing and harrowing are done and
that his cattle are in from the bad weather.

"May Jesus who died on the Cross have no
hard feelings against you my son" he says,
gently prodding the air, as if his eleven cattle
are there in front of him.

It's terrible to walk with a man who prays
like that; a man who has done his purgatory;
a man who will carry his cross into eternity.
Am I to be ravaged, too, by eternity?

* The Author acknowledges kind permission from the Editor, *The Lilliput Press* www.lilliputpress.ie to use some verbatim references therein to John's father, Jimmy.

THE KING OF ALL THE BIRDS

When my world is falling apart,
I go looking for you –
troglodytes troglodytes troglodytes.

Your moves are elusive – you become
A presence and that's it: you are there
As if from nowhere.

When you come to my tree, your
Shrill voice is silent, as we each observe
The other with an inscrutable dignity.

You are the epicenter of equilibrium –
One false move from you and
Everything could diverge.

Your tiny heart enters mine; your
Beady eye and pert tale: the gyroscope
That stops me spinning.

THE IRISH MIND
to Ivor Browne

Celtic images prevail
In your Mandala of the brain:
Spiral forms on granite rocks –
Glaucous eyes with which we
See our labyrinths of the past:
Early aubade to Auden's Maze.

And now those pagan symbols
Of yesteryear are no more:
When joy was a *kind of* yeast, the
Fungous ferment of an unleavened
World; and the provenance of
Uncircumspect deities.

*

On Dalkey's adamantine structure
– Reliquary of pristine persons –
Listening – scallop-like – to a new
Silence of Meaning, a unique
Consciousness was formed in you:
An older meaning of Asylum, and a

New understanding of borderlines.
Boundaries, peripheries, gateways:
Each person's individual pathway
To redemption. The penumbra –
Adam's shadow – would still remain;
Not as a demon, but as a consequence

To be explained by self, to oneself.
You taught how to lay a head on a
Pillow (not to sleep) but to release
Undead demoniacs and impel them,
Screaming, to search for some other
Unlatched door.
You proffer no denouement – only
Expanding horizons.

PAINTERLY REFLECTIONS
on The Life and Passion of Christ

1.

Was it the *Happy Family*
By Murillo: everyone
Beaming with delight,

Or Lorenzo Costa's
More sombre view
Of Reality, in which

He, who made the sun, moon and
Stars to shine so radiantly, is unable
To concede even the tiniest smile.

That black on top of grey
Canvas by Rothko says it all:
How finely balanced our fate

Is: the hairs on our head –
Numbered. Be acquainted
With Grief then as He was;

The blackbird will still
Sing its song and the wren
Dart around the brambles.

2.

How little we know
Of His life
Before thirty;

I see Him as
Introverted and
Withdrawn;

Austere, like
Luis de Morales' portrait
Of *Jerome in the Wilderness*.

And then the
Rosebud opens:
He is tactile;

The poor touch the
Hem of His garments;
He restores sight

With spit and soil;
The desolation of humanity
Is safely within Him.

3.

He becomes Paul Klee's
Golden Fish;
He is transfigured.

Out of the Ocean
Of Eternity, Man
And Destiny meet.

He allows Mary
Wash His feet and dry
Them with her hair.

That "pouring bowl"
Held by John
Over His head in

Piero Della Francesca's
The Baptism of Christ – how
Preternaturally it is

Suspended over
The White Christ in
A white cloth.

4.

In the Darkness
Reinhardt's *Invisible
Cross* can be

Seen; obliquely
We view it. He
Saw it with the

Clarity and
Equanimity of
An eagle's eye.

Mantegna's and
Bellini's *Agony
In the Garden*:

Respectful. He is
Alone in
His World;

Alone with
Our earthly
Pain.

5.

Paul Klee's *Images
Of Death*: the
Minimal man

Stripped bare;
The sardonic
Smile that

Spells Death –
The Final
Solution.

He prays "Father forgive
Them for they
Know not what they do."

Then, Resurrection
Through the palest of
Hockney's blue membranes:

We see Him descend
And Ascend through an
Eternal Light.

THE FOOL'S STOOL

He sat on it
Everyday
At eventide:

A Rodin figure
Crouched
In a posture

Of forgetfulness;
Unscrambling
The moments

Of decision,
Indecision;
Faking the

Subjects of
Desire and
Lust

To seem as
Lessons
In objectivity.

GOLDFINCH

Showy. Wanting to be seen. That's clear.
But, there I go again with my sterile attributions.

What if you are simply another ordinary bird?
Ignore that guy Swedenborg and his visions.

Forget Dicler too and his beauty equation.
Remember this 5.5 inch bird was once a dinosaur!

I look up What's that Bird –
Utters a tinkling call
Song is rapid and twittering
Nest is beautifully woven from moss & animal hair.

I leave it perched on the dead head of a teasel plant.
What's that Bird again – not bothered by human presence.

THE SCYTHE

It is, I think,
An instrument to
Play music on

Whilst cutting grass.
Music, which only
The mower can hear.

The scherzo, or whatever,
Is interrupted now and again,
To transverse

The upturned blade
With a bobbin-shaped stone
In rhythmic movements

Which replenishes the bright
Steel to inveigle the wavering
Grasses to play on and on.

And so on.

BLUE BLUE BALLOON

Three gulps of breath were thrust
into the neck of a piece of bulbous

Rubber; the neck then knotted tight
and string attached to assist gravity;

In a singular act of creation
a new universe was born.

*

Mine to hold on to; but a tactile tautness
was exciting my young, searching fingers.

I saw ultra-marine seas and cobalt blue
skies shimmer in my outstretched hands;

An inner filament was brimming my brain
to over-trip on incandescence.

*

A pin prick did it: pierced my newly-
made universe in a single, deliberate act.

I recovered the torn pieces to learn
a cruel lesson in human wilfulness.

Now you can look for it deep in Ursa Major –
twirling on the right index finger of Callisto.

TINTINNABULATION

Bells – metal cups of assonance,
Rhythmic rhymers of greeting
And farewell;

Clanging the ether with iron fists,
Numbing preoccupation, perambulation;
Galvanizing a solemn response
To craven idol's graven images.

Take me to a Holy Mountain apart,
Where I may soar above the judder;
Whose misshapen bells displace evil
Spirits and ring within my very core.

YONDER

He had a way of *seeing things*:
A hair-like movement
On the water
Was a salmon moving upstream;
A blackbird defending territory
Was a ruse.

On a walk with him
You realised a certain blindness
In oneself.
To *see yonder*,
As Hopkins spoke of,
Became a yearning.

I thought of him
When watching my mother die:
That inaudible click one sees,
–Not hears –
At the moment of death.
Look – he cried. I saw her go.

ARCANE

Because she is mute, Nature mourns – Walter Benjamin

To hear the cry of an otter at night is
      disturbing.

I do not want to hear it again.

Joseph Fagan

MUSE 4

MUSE 4

Man is the measure of all things – Protagoras

A Pharaoh's tomb:
Euclidian
All apex
Abstracted reality;
Home of the psychopomp.

No burning of the body here;
No souls set out to sea;
Preserved, contained within:
His symbol covering his Self.

Why leave this mark on sand
For all to see?
A god is buried there.

A LA RECHERCHÉ DU TEMPS PERDU

Standing – as always –
at the meeting point of two
Eternities – one past; the other yet to come,

I look in a mirror and see you
– clichéd stuff, I know –
But, today, we are both seventy one years old.

I reach out to touch your face. You do not
move but a nervous quiver of recognition

Around about your mouth, informs me you
are aware of my presence.

*

Your being here
reminds me of wintertime:
Your large hands over the fire's brightest

Flame to warm the corpuscles of our tiny feet;

To come: pint volumes of your blood given
to our waxen mother
– your body plumbed to hers –

Almost gone following a botched hysterectomy.

Tulips from Amsterdam was on the radio then –
she, singing along in bed; aglow with new life:

Looking quizzically into a hand-held mirror.

AN IRISH DRUID ASKS THE TREES TO ELECT A KING*
i.m. Seamus Heaney 1939-2013

He asks the Sessile Oak to be King:
I am already king of the forest,
I am the tallest tree in the kingdom;
Ships made from my timber have conquered the world.
Also, I am sacred to Zeus, king of the gods;
Listen to the rustling of my leaves to hear the gods speak.
Enter through doors made of my wood to ward off evil spirits.

He asks the Goat Willow to be King:
I am mostly water;
I cure the headaches of mankind;
Panniers made from my osiers carried
The dried turf home from Toner's bog.
I grow best in rough & disturbed ground.
I regenerate myself if burned to the ground.

He asks the Thorn Tree to be King:
I am the most pitiable of trees;
I bend with the wind;
But, left on my own in a field, I protect the dead.

A saviour who claimed to be an Eternal King
wore a crown made from my spine-like thorns;

I am close to the earth; with a tiny spark
I could set the world on fire.

On hearing this, the Druid accepted the Thorn Tree as King.

* *Based on Judges 9 – Abimelech tries to be King and is resisted by Jotham who quotes to the people a poem about various trees being asked to elect a king. All refuse except the thorn-bush.*

JOURNEY TO ITHACA

Oars fashioned by your hand
are hung now in the garage:
left there in remembrance
as things needed by the dead
are left in a mausoleum.

Upend our long boat again on
the river bank; ignite a fire from
uniform pieces of dry wood
under a barrel of raw pitch.

Use a rounded brush to slobber
sizzling hot tar all over the
boat's bloated belly. Slowly
let it harden fast.

Listen then my dear father for that
      familiar lapping against the planks.
            The oars are out; the tiller steady in
                  my shaky right hand.

CASTAWAY

Wait till the anger goes away – then you
can deliberate. She has a *modus vivendi*
which empowers her –

Leave her with it. Look closer at
Les bâtes de la Mer by Matisse –
the one you copied so faithfully –

Re-invent like he did: scissoring
out shapes and images into new
collages of wonder and destiny.

Let the sea cucumbers, sea horses
and seaweed lead you into a world
where, perhaps, soul is unheeded.

LIFE IS A CAROUSEL

Wurlitzer music was propelling metal-horses
around in circles on that special day
in glorious La Baule.

Both of you astride a metal beast –
each on her own high-winged Pegasus,
coated in the blood of Medusa but with

Lightsome hearts of Ruhr steel that seemed
to rise and fall on cue as willing agents of an
unseen organ-grinder.

Two young hearts enthralled; we, in dread
of the moment the
music would *inevitably* STOP.

PIER AT SPIDDAL, CO. GALWAY

A wailing wall in a place where
paucity *itself* sustains the land?

I am *become undone*.

No rhetoric can save me.

I cover my eyes and walk backwards;

Imagine a land flowing with milk & honey.

ROSA LADY ARDILAUN

In your walled garden
A simple tag bears your name:
Rosa Lady Ardilaun.

When growth is dormant
A glint of metal flashes and
Identifies you.

Come Summer,
Lemony-white roses form in
Clusters around your name.

Words oscillate; a plethora
Only one term *Anglo-Irish*
Will accommodate.

But yet, you always had the look
Of one whom love eluded; here
You seem to be at peace.

MY PATERNAL GT GRANDFATHER FEGAN'S GRAVE RE-VISITED
There are spirits dread in that region wild – Speranza

Stone and bone are all that's left of you –
An upright headstone
as perpendicular now
as when it was settled into Moyglare's earth
In Loving Memory of Rosanna Fegan
who died before you in 1875, aged 64 years.

You, John, died four years after her in 1879 –
From Old Age – it's so recorded.
Born in 1796 when a Mad King
reigned and Lord Nelson was
busy losing an eye in Corsica.
But now, inquisitive cows look curiously
over a fence to where you lie, yards away.

I tell them that your dead atoms
circulate around here no more.
They keep staring at me
as I vigorously scour your
headstone to remove well-settled lichen ;
pick out things, both living and dead,
obscuring significant letters and numerals,
as my seventy year old arms ache.

I'd happened upon your Death Certificate:
Occupation – a Herd; unable to read or write.
Tabhair misneach dom a Dhia! – Courage, Lord! –
Courage to forgive those who dispossessed
my people; whose bones cry out for redress.
And you John – in the meanwhile – enjoy the
company of the Devonshire Villiers Tuthills
& their ilk in the Church of Ireland, Moyglare.
Share in peace what your family once owned.

THE MUSIC OF TERROR

Listen to Gorecki:

When it snows, the snow is black ...
I had a feeling the huts were still warm ...
"Mama, don't cry" – girl's writing on cell wall ...

Gorecki transmutes all of this into music for
Our ears to hear; we can only profess horror.

But the evening sky still fascinates us.
The next morning our sun will rise again.

TOUCHSTONE

That goddamned oil-stone block of yours
– like something from the earth's deep core –
that I so envied and which you kept hidden.

Ebony black and with a concave belly from
from your running blades and chisels over it
to transform them into "good as new".

That was you all over: never could afford
much; never bought anything you couldn't
afford. And then I go and lose it!

THE SIGHT OF DEATH

There's an hour of dread for human souls – Speranza

A man is running away
In Poussin's painting *A Man Killed by a Snake*,
Warning a washerwoman
Not to look.

A backwards glance is oblique:
Crazed that she will see a blackened
Body in full possession
Of a snake.

All else –
Images of Arcadian bliss:
Fishermen preparing their nets,
Large buildings made to last.

*

You talked about death; what Bonheoffer
Said about winning *hard grace* –
not taking the easier option
Of *soft grace*;

Of his brother's riposte –
*don't waste your life
on such a poor, feeble, boring and bourgeois
endeavour.*

Just like what you did –
Worn-out-body on a stiff white sheet –
Nuns singing *Salve Regina* – burial in 2012
In Bluebell *black-flu* cemetery.